CW00503463

SHEAF

133 & 134

WINTER 2022 / 2023

GUEST EDITOR
KELVIN CORCORAN

GENERAL EDITOR
TONY FRAZER

Shearsman magazine is published in the United Kingdom by
Shearsman Books Ltd
P.O. Box 4239
Swindon   SN3 9FL

Registered office: 30–31 St James Place, Mangotsfield, Bristol BS16 9JB
(this address not for correspondence)

www. shearsman.com

ISBN 978-1-84861-813-8
ISSN 0260-8049

Subscriptions and single copies

Current subscriptions – covering two double-issues, each 100–110 pages in length – cost £17 for delivery to UK addresses, £23 for the rest of Europe (including the Republic of Ireland), £25 for Asia & North America, and £28 for Australia, New Zealand and Singapore. Longer subscriptions may be had for a pro-rata higher payment. Purchasers in North America and Australia will find that buying single copies from online retailers there will be cheaper than subscribing, especially following the recent drastic price-rises for mail to the USA and the Antipodes. This is because copies are printed locally to meet orders from online retailers, and thus avoid the international mail. Following recent changes to the handling of cross-border transactions in the EU, purchasers in the EU (apart from those in Ireland) are recommended to use online retailers within the EU, or the UK's Book Depository, which can handle the new system.

Back issues from nº 63 onwards (uniform with this issue) cost £9.95 / $17 through retail outlets. Single copies can be ordered for £9.95 direct from the press, post-free within the U.K., through the Shearsman Books online store, or from bookshops. Issues of the previous pamphlet-style version of the magazine, from nº 1 to nº 62, may be had for £3.50 each, direct from the press, where copies are still available, but contact us for a quote for a full, or partial, run.

Submissions

Shearsman operates a submissions-window system, whereby submissions may only be made during the months of March and September, when selections are made for the October and April issues, respectively. Submissions may be sent by mail or email, but email attachments are only accepted in PDF form. We aim to respond within 3 months of the window's closure, i.e. all who submit *should* hear by the end of June or December, although we do sometimes take a little longer.

This issue has been set in Arno Pro, with titling in Argumentum.
The flyleaf is set in Trend Sans.

Contents

Peter Riley

from 'Proof...'

Proof that the world exists. Crossing Europe
in the backs of lorries, the noise of the engine,
the road rolling under, deeper by night.
Occasional glimpse of an urban skyline
changing lorries before dawn. Proving
that the world is, but unstable: the Refugee's story.
I usually wake up about four to half past
and don't go back to sleep again until after five.
I lie there listening. And it is through
this hole in the night that the wren sings.

*

The wren sings a series of single-pitch rows, usually
five to nine notes long, decorated with curlicues.
Some of these "notes" are tight clusters or quick calls
interspersed with short rows of chirps, a slide or two
and finally the "tell-tale machine-gun rattle" which
tells the tale of the Refugee's journey across Europe,
a sonorous black hole day after day.

*

Doubt that the world will continue. She doesn't
rest long, she flits upstream and perches
on somebody else's ribcage. First light slowly
infiltrates the bushes where the wren lives,
beyond the canal, whispering widths
of hope to the immediate vicinity,
realised currently as white blossom.

*

How eagerly then my tongue ran off with me
to the far edges of visibility,
where the red flower becomes symmetrical
and plunges into the ground. Where
the light traversing the day is refracted down
to the green spread, the housing of what is.
At a far edge of urban tension the Refugee
hands over €500 cash to get him from Italy
into Switzerland invisibly.

*

Half my life I sang in death's anthem
and played death's bones, why should it
bother me now? – always before us,
inhabiting and sealing the moment in its harmony,
completion and fullness of the world
inscribed on its cist. How do you get mortal harmony
out of a stone box into the moving air?
With ash and ink, and sing a lyric air with passion.

*

The Refugee in a sleeping-bag on a steel floor
opens his eyes on darkness and wonders
did he remember before he left to visit
the old holm oak up the fields, to hold
its spiked leaf in his hand and listen
to what it said? Go, it said, go now.
I'll be with you, I'll let you know
when we're on the sea.

*

The vast dark history that trails behind the route,
the great lamentation stretched across the western land-mass
for the fall of Constantinople, Dufay 1454, a version
still sung in Greek villages. And the local text,
for whomsoever is lost. *Whomsoever is here,*
Whomsoever is there, Whomsoever is
everyone you ever cared about
hidden in what's left of the world
and where are they now?

Lucy Hamilton

The Laughing Child

Inspired on seeing that both trigrams signify Fire
thus completing the hexagram to symbolise Brightness

I remind myself that the random never cheats
or lies but can be a paradox| as every truth

has its opposite which is also true| those two
sun dogs I once saw from a Greyhound in the desert

was a mirage like magic| a ruse of physics| a visible
trick by the invisible| Now as I glue my photo

of the two girls in Kun costume| their beauty
radiates over Water Lily Lake by the Pavilion

where the brightness of sunset will fall slowly
or *come of a sudden*| The law of completion

is the law that a vacuum will fill with light
or dark just as an extreme will flip to its inverse

The way a laughing child can burst into tears
or the dog Tiangu eat the sun during an eclipse

Angel Wing

I
At Ni Yan Tai Park a man in a boat swings a long wooden pole
releasing yellow fish-feed in an arc of glittering sun-lit specks

It rises and extends| a crescent moon in flight across the lake
and something in the fisherman's skilled movement conjures

a thought of Vincent and *Sower with Setting Sun*| How the stride
of the legs and the sower's seed-sling chime with the pictogram

of 'Great Man' holding a bow across his body| which in turn
summons a vision of arrows flying in multiple surging waves

II
These swans flying over the lake in a V formation appear as darts
reflecting how beauty and injury can coexist as cost exacted by gift

the way Frida Kahlo's face and antlers counterpoint the arrows
piercing her poor dear little deer body which oozes dark blood

from multiple wounds| the way Huang's will to survive his death-
sentence was inspired by meditating on the constancy of change

Some say that the disease stripping this swan's wing-feathers
stems from the glut of white bread we throw at the water's edge

Mr Gan's Studio

Noting the six broken lines of this hexagram
which symbolises Earth responding to Heaven

I trace the compound ideogram| painting
the vertical stroke in thin vermilion ink

trying to keep my brush pressure even
for the *long streak cutting through the field*

but it's not easy *to extend limited experience*
Take that afternoon at Mr Gan's studio

viewing the Master's galleries| his signature
Blue and White porcelain| then sitting among

his professional artists in paralysed trepidation
watching for clues before daring to dab a dish

gingerly adding a drop of water and tipping
neither too much nor too little| until time

and texture fused and I had three plates ready
for glazing| A willow| a poem and a jazzman

Angelina D'Roza

Correspondences: The Lark Ascending

I would tell you about the composer, who worked on his *Lark*
before and after a war, that between those years, between the original
and its revision, he drove a military ambulance. That each alteration
pasted over the previous notes, erased that old reality, as though
it never happened. Which of course, it didn't. Or Schafer's composition
of snow, his sketches of snowdrifts crossing a stave like memory traces
sung and settling through the winter trees. There's comfort
in the weight of snow, the voices that layer and hum, a sudden dark
as they open their mouths – *ah*. All this time I've been waiting for dawn
when I already had what I needed. Do you want to hear how trauma
transforms the freedom of a lark? This lark that's so in love with the land.
Perhaps the violin is the bird. The piano is the earth. The intervals
between them like an expanse of air that grows, diminishes,
equivocates. Or is the lark a projection of the earth's subliminal self,
a haunting without significance beyond this reaching upwards?

On Listening to
My Baby's Taking Me Home by Sparks

A house in which rain does not fall, a place in which spears are not feared, as open as if in a garden without a fence around it. (Irish; author unknown; 9th C)

Home, like a ritual. Like a hat taken off, head lowered at the back step, my breath held to hear the song more clearly. A sort of peace in the repeated word falling as leaves on the mat. I am exposed to its element, even as I try to shape this word to stone so carefully in my mouth. To dovetail my feet into the floorboards, the lights gone on like the ink flourish of a signature. And then someone, blown in, the altered note that unsettles walls, uproots joists, that makes what was ordinary exquisite.

A sudden blackbird on the broken trellis
its broken song flowering here
and here, one repeated lyric unconsciously

beautiful like the clematis that returns
each year with no idea of how glad I am

In asking you to love it, I am, of course, asking you to love me, though that word loses meaning the more it's used, while the song only grows more eloquent. Is this loss what happened to *god*? Like the Vikings minting Christian coins and spelling St Petri with Thor's axe, as though the rise of one religion and the demotion of another to mythology met in quivering peace. Here too, there's repetition, the notion of god continuous even as it changes, while the word *god* stays the same. But if there's a parallel of attenuation between the language of god and love, isn't there also our desire to be held, to be home, to lower our gaze and read intentionality into the soil?

Correspondences: Oak

after James Canton

With each ending, he returns to the ancient oak
until he is, perhaps at last, alone. He talks about sailing
too far from the tree, and I think this anchoring
                    saves him. He's telling me what I need
though I'm aware of how much I'm looking
exactly for this.
                        The comfort is in the illusion
of constancy. Or, is it in the seasonal, the falling, again?
You touch my arm as you walk by. By this
I mean only to register an encounter
                            which is how we mean at all.

*

Think of the canopy as delimiting this space
where such an encounter is possible. Under its cover
the conditions provide the ghost life
of bats and birds
                    that would, he says, have been here
had all the oaks survived.
When you slip your hand into my pocket
                                when I let you
we open a dialogue both with each other and
with these ghost birds, the bullfinch
                    lamenting the morning sun.

*

                    Not constancy, then, but longevity.
That's what he's saying about *oak knowledge*.
To rest a hand on the tree and feel its outlasting calm
the slow rhythm of eight-hundred years.

13

To mark time with the turning inwards in snow
                         the dismantling of leaves.
Are we changed in this, exposed as we are?
             What is this need to hold my body
against something more lovely
                         against more than myself?

*

I've become aware of the disconnect between my body
and the stories it tells. I am dominated by
                         and change the oak
the way a nesting owl lines its tree hole
         alters the surrounding air with its call.
But an owl that thinks itself tree. Tells tree stories.
                         Grows to the shape of the wind.

*

What do we want from each other, if not each other, *each oak's own oakness?*

*

The oak reading is mapped against the recomposing
of Vivaldi's *Spring*. It is possible to talk about this
                 in the same terms as the tree
how the composer had to see the music, feel the strings
                 as though they were his own
to meet them, suddenly
be moved by them, before he could transform them.
                 Not equals, but there was love.
The ways we leave each other changed
         a violin phrase caught in the branches.

Aonghas Macneacail

sùisinis 1996

i, present here, alone
have human breath to
offer sùisinis
this pale gray afternoon
the wind is silent;
over there the sea's asleep,
the cuillin's great saw masked

but here, where there were
céilidhs, quarrels, courtships, still
the mason's measured art remains
while hearths are air-conditioned,
thatch and thatcher long absorbed
into the turf, the singing wheel
which span at summer doors
is air, is memory, the stories
of old voyages, from
lochlann and from gaelic south
which married here, have long since
put on threadbare coats and left,
those tweeds which took their colours
from the rocks and leaves did not
go willingly their dumb inheritors
(still numerous) have nothing much to say –
a cough, a bleat, a cropped appraisal
of sweet grass, shrugged fleece, while
there an eyeless shepherd's house
still wears its iron hat, red, furrowed, dropping
rust into a skewed and swollen mattress
which sinks through the broken bed as if
a ship of scaffolding gone down were
dragging this dark porous reef, its nemesis

and as i walk among stone vacancies
the ghosts i call on stay indoors, while
on these shaven grazings, any questions
from my pocket radio discusses how
it's cheaper to feed blood and bone
to herbivores

eternal

resting his tender head between her thighs
as if to listen for the heartbeat of

                             no longer there

its journey out
                  from a dark and confidential sea
                  into the singing air

                  how life drew rivers from a hill

how light became

                  embroidered motion of an insect dancing

memories

                  fall like rain   into the sea

mapping warm beginnings
still,

    after all these years

                  the mystery of flesh
                  and pulse and exhalation

read it again
in the honey cave
braille dancer

        touch, but there can be no finding
        centre
        yet   ever

only tentative
kindness, love, desire
          the curious   eternal

gaudy jane

o gaudy jane, you are my window on the night,
through you I've watched chiaroscuro turning bright,
the dullest day has blossomed into wild excursions
through deep neon forests where kaleidoscopic fruit
become a warm fermenting sea of joy,
but should I find myself alone, I know you'll people me
with dancing voices, laughing feet, bare shoulders, ecstasy,
tonight you are a head of liquid corn and your singing
will not cease and in that dizzy latticework of sound
all words are prodigal

o gaudy jane, you are the glass that parts my lips
in thirsty speech, you lend me the eloquence of your arm,
your lifelong consonantal drumbeat's hammering
abseils from the bated walls of the room
where we dance,
and I have no head for heights,
but should you lead me to the pinnacle
I'll still be anchored in my reef of straw
below
for I have drunk your golden fire

o gaudy jane, you are my door into the meadows
of grandiloquent suns, where the unspoken flows
on seed-rich trade of glances – I'm drunk with you
who dance your long mad dance in this,
my whisky trance,
and all the time I'm here your spilling fingers
play wild flutes on me,
and in those liquid falls of light, you radiate
each single match to flame, ember, candle,
spark that sets all breath alight

o gaudy jane, you only ever come
to me at this late hour,
and always in the crowded rooms where secret
words are butterflies your eyes are luminous
shoals,
hinted, random, spilling, drops and
stains of paint, yet still the deepest
and most true, those candid affirmations,
pure bright orange spears of light
twin goddesses of sabotage

o gaudy jane, I see your breast become a ball of chequered tweed
from which my lips can draw out neither milk nor gall
just marsh and weed you the flesh of all the janes
and now you strip each veil away
that fading joseph coat of fog falls all around
your hands that beckoned me
have gone the colour of all cavern night;
and now I am a ghost among the crowd
I see your silk dress in the golden moonlight
with the rainbows woven into it
and will dream of your lips of fire forever more
my gaudy love

Gordon Alexander

In Pure Heart

The lamplight of remorse, in a dull ring
Little like gold, I shall not put away,
Hoping that if I never cease again
To struggle with a heartbroken chimaera,

Struggle of blood and tears, as it wounds
And savages me in a pure demise,
My own as well as that of a fond dream,
I might one day return to Fontainebleau

No longer found in rotten canvases,
The Fontainebleau of old layers of brown,
Like paper or rags, as when I in love
Found my antique betrothal in some attic.

New Awareness of Light

Some time ago, when I wasn't dying of lead-poisoning and the keening
of a fly, as I like to think of my rotten interior when holding a gentian –
I sometimes call it, that rotten interior, the Mystery of the Green Coffers
which, I hardly need add, were locked and rumoured to have been cursed by
a diabolic cult of sailors who, scarcely escaping death, pledged themselves
forever to sickness and the Leichnam-divinity –, I found some kind of
purpose in ruining a wing of rarefied oak with the foul blood of mistletoe
and fruiting ivy. But since the light of a declining dawn appeared to me,
not even the ruins of thought – not even in a dim curiosity like that of a
dying figure like Napoleon, in the green mansions abandoned above the
sea, held there for some unknown reason, for he is lesser than Napoleon,
though still the holder of a notable office – detain the one who, as though
dead, cannot understand beauty: words are no longer sufficient; their

charms are not equal to those of a Chardin, or a Rembrandt; his learning has already risen beyond the reach of words, and almost beyond that of music, and yet he can still hardly read, his various vocabularies, ancient and modern, still somewhat limited. There is nothing that can be done: of the world, which contained the Hermitage, the Musée du Louvre, he can recall only a discoloured mop in a bucket, in some kind of courtyard – a sort of coalhouse of brick, covered in calcareous plaques and accretions, can be seen behind it – which used to be interesting, vaguely reminiscent of a Corot, but isn't interesting any more.

The Ecstasy of Lyric

I sometimes find myself in the position of opponent to the crumbling Amor, his face washed off, author of all that is petty and deceitful. His smile as though lost in flannel belies the eternal acts of corruption that Orpheus fundamentally fails to grasp.

Only when I learnt of the vicious motives of the wasp Anteros did I acknowledge love's golden, marble-floored sun. It is spacious and lonely, and the heart predominates; my thought is full of empty recitations. I walked burdened with the year, a small temple of Apollo consulted often, late at night, under the dreary lamp. Each day I found through some door, presumably mine, the unchanging bed of defeat, the cat long-departed to the bronze-sunned cities, black with heat. I sensed the dismal practices of our foe, the embittered, amphora-headed Mesembria, but my shield was riddled with grief.

There is no defence against the philosophical depths, out of which sick Amor, his ancestor the unmoving Dis, has understood the days that required no meaning. Wandering vipers dropping from him, his alchemical interpretation of life is satisfying to lovers and deposed priests obsessed with ennui.

Determined to prove life meaningless without love, or something like that, he breaks into the old corridor, experienced in everything as he approaches the lonely door of calm Hypnos. It is now, under the sword of the murderer, white-winged like love, that peace shall become hideous like the endless humming of an insect, and our long sense of purpose dies in a rotten corner, like a city where dogs run like obsessed sleeves over a cemetery.

Geraldine Clarkson

from The Vitalist Sees the Signs

The Vitalist Creams Off the Prophets

The vitalist is not crude, and has a full head of sublimations: from Amos to Zechariah, she knows her stuff. She eyes up Isaiah, handles Hosea, and has an octobrach broken tongue which crumbles like butterbread if she comes out with truth and wise saws. Biting back deeper matter, she's sore.

The Vitalist Finds Employment in a Funeral Parlour

where, in a back room, she helps devise new merchandise, 'Ashes to Casserole Dishes', 'Departed Fistbumps', grief crystals for the bath—*Relax Relics*—and other dead-friendly ventures. She fantasises about a *Lock-it Locket* wearable key— which secures a door you never want to open again. Her bosses are impressed and though she works for a sub-living wage, without holiday or sick pay, there are posthumous perks, and a coffin thrown in. Also use of the garage as a gym when it is empty.

Treadmill of the dead.

The Vitalist Endures a Winter's Tale

Lost, she then loses everything she has, as a kind of revenge. She loses her parents, her siblings, her children, co-workers, home, country, dentist. She is cold and angry and the wind burns her naked and icy, but quite dry, and she bokes a winterword.

The Vitalist Escapes Purgatory

There, that wasn't that hard, was it.

The Vitalist Re-Reads Page 263,

and, this time, cries.

The Vitalist Goes Vile

Vile vile to market
and buys spider crabs
vile vile home again
to scald them and scold them
for dire webby flesh
and for failing to attend
to a deep green book
with seascape frontispiece

The Vitalist Meets Katherine Mansfield and They Prepare Great Party Food Together

Baked eggs, apricots and cream, cheese straws; anchovies. Black coffee. Mirabelle. Whiskey. De-crusted sandwiches layered with lemon curd, marmalade & handsome gooseberry jam. Elderflower jelly. Brown-speckled fish flounces. Whipped cream puffs, stacked shakily high. Orange soufflé. Coldwater scones with plentiful butter. A basket of berries. Tiny blue saucers of redcurrant jelly. Whole celestial cheeses. Limes. Gold plums. Hare soup. Stuffing balls. Platters of ham. Masses of mustardy rolls, spruced with spider crab.

The Vitalist Wades Through a Bog of Misogyny

a stinkhorned off-white mess like sour cream, hiding stinging
fish and sinkholes, a whole sucking morass between her and the
next milestone, a whole smirking mire.

The Vitalist Visits the Dead Zones of the Sea

Having been given an index, she set out to log each one; a
mourner-tourist, three-hanky mariner, with no skill to reverse,
only to observe and record, and wail internally. She tries psychic
healing. Children murmur, mermaids cheer.

Lucy Maxwell Scott

Rosa Argues with Leo in Ten Letters

February 1894, Paris
I am here, defining Polish industrial development. But you are not writing your paper. I write many articles for the Cause. You tell me nothing of the Cause. I beg for news like sugared almonds. Not a word from you. And the Russians? What of the Russians? Do not imagine that a 'sweetheart' thrown into the mix of your words makes your withholding more palatable?

March 1894, Paris
My concierge is engaged flagrante with an undercover agent. At night I smell her violet perspiration. I hear her whispering while I write for you and the Cause. You are not here.

April 1894, Paris
I have destroyed your letters as the bitch downstairs may yet denounce me. Why are you not here?

June 1898, Berlin
My mother is dead, and yet still you take your pen and ride furiously through my lines, striking out this and that. I thank you for the lessons, for the many important mistakes you have brought to my attention. Will you not fix the matter of your citizenship?

July 1898, Berlin
Do I love you? Yes, yes, yes. With the violence of a swan. But first I shall prove that capitalism must break its neck.

September 1898, Berlin
Today I am dressed in the jaunty yellow jacket I have purchased. I throw back your demand that I wait for your guidance. You demand I hold German politicians in my pocket, seduce nations, bring forth a revolution, but still fear that without your presence I will purchase the devil knows what.

December 1898, Berlin
Undercover agents loiter by my basement, spit tobacco, suffocate the air with the musk of their aspirations. They chat idly with the janitor while their eyes follow me through windows and out onto the street. Every step they are there. And where, my love, are you?

January 1899, Berlin
Why must you dismiss every Russian, every Russian sentiment, as irrelevant or counter to our Cause? What does it achieve to create your own Siberia, freeze the life out of the revolution for the failings of the few?

January 1900, location unknown
If I wish to go to the dogs, I will. I and my words will steal out and mingle with the multitude. And you? On what grounds do you hound and harangue me? With what books do you imagine yourself the teacher and I the troublesome pupil? Every dog has his day, and today is no longer yours.

May 1900, Berlin
You have charged in again on your high horse, your pen slicing through till you have decimated the reluctant Poles. Remember. We agreed. We will not attack. We will raise their desire for the Cause with words. I am disturbing Catholic meetings, crowding halls, enticing in the bourgeoisie. Leave all of this to me.

Perhaps the Land

Found poem; The Mass Strike, the Political Party and the Trade Unions (1906),
by Rosa Luxemburg

Changeable phenomenon
      reflects all. The struggle flows,
a broad billow over the whole.
It divides.
      It bubbles forth
as a fresh spring,
completely lost

under strikes, mass strikes, partial
strikes, demonstrative
strikes, fighting strikes, general strikes.
Peaceful
street massacres
run side by side
      flow in and over
ceaselessly
moving
living pulse-beat
      of the revolution.

In Britain
it has not been possible.
Bourgeois   struggles
between frogs and mice in stagnant waters,
unorganised
      worst organised
         totally unorganised.
Who will develop
the miners,
the textile workers,
and perhaps the land?

Eliza O'Toole

Abscission

I

I remember the heat and the cows, and the shimmers in between, and the cows' pats and their halos of flies, their crusts, and the warm belch of the dairy herd, all piss and shit. I remember the field, the divots and the sandy soil, the places where limbs lay fallen and the nettles, the damp depressions puddled by the herd, the rings of field mushroom the size of plates under the drip line of the big old horse chestnuts, the drunken estate railings. I remember chewing the soft white inner stems at the base of blades of lime green grass, the sweet sheath shared with the deep cherry Lincolnshire Reds; and having stung legs spiked by scratchy pasture. I remember blood. I remember Pat the Polish cowman, and his skinny sheep dog. There were no sheep, but Jess brought up the Reds for milking and they were as meek as sheep under her stare. I remember the dairy clock striking every quarter, five minutes before the church chimed. Five minutes gave the dairy herd time to be there, ready to start the milking hour. I remember the Reds swishing their tails in the dry, and the dust and the flies, and I remember the long slow, the dust motes float, and that it was five o'clock. I remember the tinder grass and high summer. The glimmer and the stink. I remember the telephone wires stretched to infinity, the thrum of endless fields of harrowed furrows. And the bombing swallows. Screaming. Sky full.

II

I remember deep damp ditches, dogwood, spindle, guelder rose, wild damson, cherry plum, crab apple, oak and ivy and my bare arms clawed by blackthorn whilst looking for wild garlic, bluebells, and Queen Anne's lace. I remember the grubbing out of hedges, the gashes, the gaping holes with trashed raw edges. I remember the stumps grinding and the chain saws. Sappy and whining. And at harvest, I remember with stricken awe, the miles and miles of burning straw. I remember streaming eyes, and the stranding: rabbits, hares, stoats, field mice. The stubble burning, the flickers of sparks and the glittering glimmerings of moths smoking. I remember choking, and the sloughing skies of pewter stoked with pink. And the shadow of a dog fox cresting the fire driven across acres and acres of smouldering stalks. And the diving pipistrelles. Echo locating. Sky full.

III

I remember the autonomous reality of the land and the loss of adhesion in the abscission layer. I remember the time of separation; I remember the fall.

Field (n.) ~~(v.)~~

between etymon and reflex

a chasm

Field (n.) (v.)

Abscission; a process of shedding, a cutting a part, a falling and a landing.

Possession; a conclusion of law, a defining of the nature of a particular relationship of control. Demonic over land. Reified.

Land: a muddle, a rooted place, a willing coalition of living. & the dead.

Cleavage; state of being cleft, being divided by force, state of separation. Land after law.

Language; a set of words set upon sand conveying dominion of land. A maker of myth.

Law; an originary violence and legitimating force in the name of a right. A holder of mythologies, a faker of truth. A contour of power, black letters, a dead hand.

Poetry; a naming and a making of names, an intercellular bridge, a disassembly, an unlimiting undeconstructible justice. Includes the non-human.

The passing of land

After the fall I learned this: this deconstructed thing has force; performative, and violent in its coup de grace, and with standing stood tall on its textual throne, reconstructing this muddy field cast now, enthralled, and incised with mystical authority; inscribed in black letters, mots of the law. Motes in the eye. Land put into words. Down. Forced as foie gras. Forced as clay. The conceit of that.

So, on. I looked for the legal tale and I found the calligraphic calf, its queasy flayed skin conveying a conceit. Limits where there are none, borders where there were none, none at all. Words with intentions. It was an etymological mining, unearthing the unstable, the foundation less, amongst the violence of words contesting meanings and in collision, scattering presence in inscription and collusion. Inter alia, ad infinitum. A tale of *taile*, a cutting apart wagging the calf.

First, I learned to deconstruct a feudal estate and to reconstruct it: *feudum talliatum*; first take make *en* and add a *taile* and make no mistake this composition has actual consequences entailing the destroying of worlds. Not a chance word, no Oulipo here; here a controlled and composed word, a dangerous amalgam, land & law, dangerous as corn & black smut.

Entail meant said our dad, that our house rented from the Manor was not really our house, twice over. Land passed. Entail was a rule about who could possess our house and when. I was ten then. Dad said that when the old Major, whose family had owned the village from time immemorial (he said) was dead, our home would be owned by the Major's oldest son whose wife wanted to have our house. The son and wife had had enough of each other, he said. It was bad. There were rumours I didn't understand. Dad said "*entail*" would be the end of her. She would be rent, he said, asunder. And we would too, soon.

Second, rather than cutting apart, I learned that a tailor sews up what is cut apart stitches, and knits up draws together gathers connects as a cutter cutting apart & sewing together inseparably, rent parts. There are consequences entailed in any cutting apart; consequences are always entailed inseparably. Blood inseparable from land, kin inseparable from skin. Entrails. Land and blood. Entailing the blood line inseparably from land and land inseparably from the blood riven in the males driven through like Skegness in candy, whilst females grew shrouded, sheathed in abscission layers. Falling, not landed.

Diffraction as Haraway   would have it. Duplicity as I have it. Entailing limits, in a word bounds land, fields a conceit where there was only the sun. Words feathered in gall, carved into calves' skin, a tale of deceit writ large as a mote

in the eye, a taile of conceit; an aporia – a tilting of a world,
renten.

&

So, on.

Bedrock

It is an error to use *rock* for a stone,
or just any out
 crop; ice polished catastrophically,
 topped by soil, stray boulders, murrain &
 graptolithus.

Only a giant can heft a rock;
a man can
hold a stone. Blackstone
could see "no foundation
      in nature or in natural law, why a set of
      words upon parchment should convey the
      dominion of land ... "   a stone in a
 hard place. Image of ship
 wrecks

in the alternative space, between lies
and rib
      rock, in large formations, even Nations as.
Sure, as that. Foundations.

Mythical as that.   Rock writ.

Not swaying, but rocking

boats slumbering,
cradled and bed rokken.

Penelope Shuttle

pretend paths
from Evening Journals

a pretend path
ebbing into golds
and menial footsteps
of dusk

*

past master of the sky

he grants your vow your wish
your request
in a hush of ankle socks

*

a tiny birth-control pineapple
hearsay of the past
the sub-lunar hands of the sky
sister ships with no ports of call

*

a silkworm spell
and some octopus cuddles

rocking a moral cradle
making a stay-at-home fuss

*

the wolf-lily's rebuke
a thistle's gift
loose ends
and tingles

*

toy worlds
all corners and mistakes
rainy versions of everything
(apricots)
a moth, postponed

*

a stint of cloud
bluffs of light
the one-sided kingdom
wardrobe dusts
the side-stepping light
a locksmithery
a keepsake bird

*

pouring the balmy sake
from an old kettle
a bird's nest
tucked
in his back pocket

*

Dad
in an off-duty moment
at the Chinese High School |Barracks
at Bukit Timah Rd Singapore

looking very young
jaunty
in his tropical uniform

(photo 1941)

*

gift of the Imperial Emperor of Japan
on the Emperor's birthday –
two pineapple chunks
for each starving prisoner of war

*

at Chungkai Camp for the *heavy sick*
the prisoners could attend lectures
history and physics
heard cricket stories

*

amber falcons
jars of honey
timber and silk
pelts of black foxes
my seahorse notebook
a oaken feasting bucket
the shapeshifters flitting
from bear to man from man to wolf
seals to women women to birds
a Frankish sword

*

a puzzle of silver animals
this iron-studded dragon

*

cheerful pruning of trees
lullabies for the newly dead
paths of the earth
dust and shadows
wonderful oblivions
a threading-needles-by-moonlight contest
half-moon paths of the earth
childhood as handprint
and heart print

*

swan among the flowers
queen of the river
                    (An Englishman's Flora, Geoffrey Grigson)

*

an anonymous galliard
from the sixteenth century
spinning a fine thread
from a star to the ear of The Virgin

*

the heart collects up its few belongings
even unto the utter ruin of delight

*

abc of the world
snails make the laws
helped by the dragonflies

*

a timeliness of beds
the many-times-read page
swans breasting the hailstorm
white on white
(this sounds better in French)

*

a hill
rolling off a postcard
into my lap

a summer lost at sea
opening a window to greet me

*

moon's mercy
in a sevenfold sky

the sun raises his right hand
swearing allegiance

*

my last good day
patchwork rain
vice-versa of silence
backlash of silence

*

bread of the blue shepherdess
a fox sparrow singing about his death
in a long-ago world

skitters of light
lulling my sleep back

Cecile Bol

Obstacles on the Yellow Brick Road

When a girl's an empty kettle

Barely vicenarian, this kettle
besought to be replenished, so iron
tracks led me to Amsterdam, off to see
an old bloke wielding obsidian hair
but not much else – had groomed him patiently
not yet knowing men rarely need grooming
by definition, I knew George Clooney
would be in town doing his tricks and went
four hours early to grant me the chance
of a more enchanting bedmate – I failed –
he took a deep drag in default attire
light-absorbing enough to be allowed
to grease me with rum and Coca-Cola –
stubborn as squeaky metal I ignored
how his pepper wouldn't hide salty roots,
thought that squinting my eyes maybe I could
believe this self-inflicted illusion
and what-the-hell let him fuck me – I lay
awake, endured snoring throughout the night,
imagined the bath scene in Out of Sight,
realised both men would never suffice –
afterwards, he wrote of love – I did not
waste any heartbeat of sadness on him.

Mr. Nice Guy

I.

If I ever meet you, don't be an idiot –
be nice, or at least approximately decent, please
don't say something racist or that you once drowned
a plastic bag full of puppies in the river, what
do I know about you anyway? – it's your word
against gossip and Google, please be nice and like me
instantly, the moment we shake hands and I say
my name and 'nice to meet you, and you are…?'
– like me enough to let your boy's heart seep through
that grown man's armour, I promise I won't tell anyone
when minutes become hours, while I do my best to follow
your cutesy-putesy English and pretend I don't smell
how you are rosemary hills in a Beaufort 4 sea wind
– you are so sexily disappointed when I eventually tell you
this must stop, this really must really stop, because
sorry sorry sorry, my marriage rolls without guilt-free fucks
it has been such a pleasure meeting you, though, kiss-kiss,
one on both cheeks, now let go of my hand, boy, goodnight!

II.

'At last, we finally meet,' I whisper in the mirror
with a wicked Bond-villain twinkle, as if my entire career
has been dedicated to steering myself towards this
exact spot in time, ha-ha-ha-ha! – or has it?
I neglected to renegotiate any extramarital pleasure –
instead I've spent the last two days catching up
on your story, well done for having such a big, long
Wikipedia entry – now my mind feels overloaded, knowing
too much, how will I succeed pretending you tell me
something new with this Basil Fawlty broken record
screaming not to mention, not to mention, not to mention

especially not the thought of tying your wrists together
and forcing you down on your knees – damn, shh now
these purring ovaries, scratching on the inside of my loins
meow-meow-meowing to be curled-up kittens in your lap
– I chose my outfit with meticulous care, not too conservative
certainly not too racy, I am a monogamous wife, I am
a monogamous wife, I am a mo-no-ga-mous wife.

III.

You are polite, your hair has been cut short
– you ask questions, but don't really listen, as if
you'd rather be at home with a beer and your feet
on the coffee table; well, don't we all, don't we all …
what's more, not once do you glance at my lipstick
or let your gaze glide past my chest – nor do I catch you
eyeing any of the other women – you annoyingly
decent creature – back in the bed of my hotel room
my version of you tells me I'm 'so-very-nice' too.

About those boys you like that aren't me

On the days you think about killing yourself
I enjoy watching you
watching them try. How they die, die, die,
but refuse to die. How you light up
when they stitch their shadows back on
– if not in this set of dimensions,
why not in another?

Sure, there's trauma,
ruptures, lacerations, crushed bones, pure
madness, but remember:
you had a professor with one arm once and
wasn't Van Gogh out of his fuckin' mind?

Damage is petrol. Jetpacks
are real things.

This is not to suggest you won't
ever die. This is to put forward life
has been expecting you,
except maybe it isn't an enemy
that's waiting for you
in a swivel chair behind a desk
petting the white Persian cat on its lap.

Tomorrow you'll cry again and again
I'll offer you my shoulder. Vacant,
unlike yours, and that would be alright
if only you'd listen.

Your crowded shoulder is a magnet
for disdead boys. They gather
on it like swallows on a power line.
Their melodies pouring into your ears
are 80s action series
in which the good guys never bleed.
Hear them chirrup: *live, live, live!*

Edward Lee

Shadows Remain

Sometimes we didn't
have time to shower
before we had to return
to our spouses, our hours
limited by the depths of the lies
told to buy that time.
Those times, our skins unclean
and yet purer
than they'd ever been,
I felt less guilty, the
smell of you
on my body
easing my conscience
when my wife asked me
how my day had been
and I lied as easily as though
my tongue had been born
to tell anything but truth.
What cruel people
we were in our love
for each other. What
cruel people we had to be
to save our love
for each other.
We wish our others well
now that we are gone
from their lives, our cruel selves
no more, now that
no false words are needed
to disguise our truth, though
their shadows remain

as such shadows always do,
like dirt on the skin
that an ocean of showers
can never remove.

Our

I lip-read our future
across your nipples,
my tongue moistening
those words that catch
in your shuddering mouth
as you guide me lower,
deeper.

Hours

Your fingers find home
as they meet
across the back
of my freshly shaved head,
guiding my tongue deeper,
stretching your soft voice louder,
capturing my name
in the nonsensical speech patterns
of passion, the star-skyed night
still young, the serious morning
still hours away.

The quickest way to a man's heart
is through his chest, breaking bone
and scattering veins and flesh,
causing a pain I have never felt

but can imagine in breath-catching detail,
especially when I am in the mood
I am in now.
Everything else – pretty words
danced across air and pages -
is just strained metaphor
boiled dry in cliched similes,
and I have no stomach
for such things, the mood
I am in.

Once We Both Know Pleasure

Your cunt spreading
around my dick,
coming home
to come, one
after the other,
or together,
it doesn't matter.
All that does
is having these moments
when we can be
the base beings
we are – purity under
another name – reveling
in the wanting
of each other,
words, panted or otherwise,
no longer needed, both of us
coming, one after the other,
or together, it doesn't matter,
it doesn't matter
once both our bodies know
the pleasure.

Finn Haunch

Northern Town

i.
This is how I imagine it, the point of no return.

Shunted through a train window: snubbed chimneys –
the fuck-you fingers of the north, that were once
warm to the touch.
                    Psalms of steam and pig-iron abide in the memory,
                              each one stubborn
                                        as a spelk.

Look up from your seat – there are kids gobbing from the footbridge.
Take note of them.
                    In the pub, once, some bloke sidled over
with a story. He told me how this viaduct,
that his grandmother saw built,
is stuffed with straw. We smoked fags in the doorway –
we drank stout, disputed its god.
                              Far above us both, dark water dampens
                                        [through the arches.

Do you know where you've found yourself — *do you really?*

ii.
Masher Dawson, my great grandfather, owned that yard down there –
he was the one who lost an arm
punching through a window, who screwed on a hook
that curled from his sleeves like
a coat hanger.
                    He butchered his own pigs, too. We kept his arm
from being chucked in the skip, you can see scratch marks
scoured on the rods. This was just another thing that people did, you
would have done them too.

44

But that yard… me and our kid
went there. We would scramble under warped
wire fences with secateurs and blunt scissors,
cut tunnels through brambles that
sprouted over the concrete.
Smashed bottles
were in the clearing; there were glue sticks, damp exercise books,
the sort of stuff that us and
our mates would make fires
with.
We sniffed the fumes together
and had visions – we were laughing
yes, but we were so
afraid.

Phenomenon

Midmorning – that plainer-than-thou protestant cloudlight
stops me, mid-swing. The axe snugs into my palms.
Three suns are overhead… greater, lesser,
greater… *this*, according to Google,
is a parhelion sundog.
Something that happens sometimes.
Midwinter – four-hundred miles upwind, on the peninsula,
the suns harden: a dog-walker, looking up, sees
a hermit with a storm lamp shuffling
over snow. Under this, ferns.
Under this, stiff grass. Under this,
a candle burning in the well.
No-one had placed it there —
the moss-dark was glimmering, and even picturing it
throws time out of mind
to here; in the dead garden, time resumes, the axe
drops.

Yorkshire Tea

In the ad-man's mind: platonic North
means brass bands, pubs and yes
Emmerdale. There's a kind old chap with
that no-nonsense manner, tweed waistcoat
and oh-so-obvious
whippet.
        He's bollocking about with a tin bath
on the slopes. That Last-of-the-Summer-Wine stuff.

To the ad-man, his tea is grown especially
in India.
        On the plantations of Assam.
Beside the royal warrant, on each box,
a watercolour from
                the dales. And then the consumer –
a rambler with a laminated map
and compass. Clamber up over the stile,
beside the pitch,
        sit on neat grass, sip
from a thermos,
        clap, politely, at the cricket.
                This is middle-class guilt.

Let me show you something else, that Loweresque
bluntness on the other
side –
        a mill town, dying off.
                Take our Jeff down there,
a father of three. Sketched with
charcoal. He bangs his boots together
at dawn, sheds clarts on his doorstep. Other
men do the exact same. The sun has not come up
yet. They really should leave soon.

Their wives, those gossipy cows in curlers, are about
to crowd the ginnels. They smoke in their dressing gowns.

'84

I think, Thatcher's firmly in power. This is the biggest
strike since '26. Jeff's missus
mumbles. The others pretend not to notice, but they do —
here, at least,

scabs get what scabs deserve. But
it doesn't matter. Soon enough, the mills are boarded up.
Tory, Labour, Tory – nothing happened,
nothing happened again and again. Knotweed broke
through the scrap yards. We would play in them as kids, have punch-ups
for fun, killing time.

The echoes were endless .

Behind the bus stop, someone's sniffing glue.

They drink tea here too.

Lisa Blackwell

Turquoise swimsuit

You are almost thirteen years old. You are in the back garden in your new turquoise swimsuit, the material of which stretches and ripples in a new way.

The sun flashes on the ripples of your father's pond. Self-built. The koi carps' startled lips gape at the surface. Their ghostly orange and white forms blurred beneath.

Your father says:
Oh that's unusual.

He pinches the material of your swimsuit and rolls it between his thumb and index finger.

All of a sudden, he has the electric-shock realisation that you, with your new woman body, are in the swimsuit. He becomes self-conscious and slightly embarrassed and retreats into the house. Mumbling something.

You laugh at him. You feel the power of your body but also its betrayal. This is not the body to shinny up a tree. Or to give your brother a dead arm.

You begin to wonder if this body is more trouble than it's worth.

Grey kitten

You are fourteen years old. You are playing with your friend's new kitten in his house. It is a grey tabby. Its claws are the very points of pins. A cloud of grey and white fright fur. You hold it crescented to your chest, barely feeling its light being, as it closes its eyes. You ask its name, to a shrugged reply.

Your friend's mum and her boyfriend come into the living room and put on a pornographic video. It is circus themed and involves clowns with very long noses. Every face a gurning mask.

You sit very still and watch. Breathing is too much movement. They don't seem to notice anyone else is there.

As the film continues, your friend has an argument with his mum's boyfriend, against the backdrop of waves of fuzzy-fleshed tv.

He asks if you want to leave.
You say:
Yes!

You place the unsteady kitten on the sofa. A tiny grey dot. For a small second as you exit, you watch it slipping on the faux-leather towards the black back.

You never see the kitten again. You ask the next time you are round, but everyone is vague about where it went.

You wonder if this is how it all works.
With all the barely-there slight things,
slipping silently into the shadows.

Batman's avatar

He wears a t-shirt with a Batman icon
emblazoned across his chest. He tells you
how shit his life is. Worn like a bruise.
A purple grave of loneliness. He makes excuses
for a man's bad behaviour. He's *not used to,*
you know, women with opinions, you know,
women that don't agree. No, you don't know.
Those women, the orange ones. You know, the ones
with the lips. You call bullshit. He presses on.
The ones with nothing to say. Essex ones.
Just want a bloke. He says he wasted

his thirties on the PlayStation. He sends
you a clip of his avatar as a cowboy
in a Western game. His avatar punches
his horse. His horse kicks him to the ground.
His avatar, floppy-armed, staggers to his feet.
The clip finishes. He tells you he is a feminist,
and when you laugh, he gets angry. *I am,*
he says, *I am. I AM.* He sends you a clip
of his avatar in a saloon dancing
drunkenly and falling over. He complains
about his neighbours upstairs. They are quiet

but their baby is always crying. Always
crying. *She really needs to get her knockers out,*
he says. You are silent. The words hang
in the air above you. He sends you a clip
from his avatar's point of view. Someone
is lying on the ground. There is a close-up
of their face. You see his avatar's hand
point a gun. Then, the face and its flat
expression is obliterated. There is white
bone, mottled red and grey viscera
across the screen. You click delete.

Jessica Bundschuh

A Mother's Court Testimony on Grief

Let's start with the grief of a burning library. Imagine a fire long ago in Alexandria: 400,000 rolls of papyrus send smoke up to Zenodotus, the first librarian who weeps and casts a curse at the furies. One summer I watch a three-week trial just to hear the victim's mother finally say: *when a daughter dies, a library burns.* Then the court reporter reads back to her testimony about a drilling hammer that bludgeons a skull and a pocketknife that pierces a throat, and this mother, who actually is a librarian, admits to neglecting the librarian's mantra for survival: classify, catalog, edit. *What's memory left with,* she asks coolly, *if it can't scavenge what's lost?* like the Egyptians who made foreign ships wait in their port for copies their *own* manuscripts. Handwritten anew, their scribes licked thin inky reeds, bruised and frayed from abuse, which brings us to the end, with summer fires hotter each year. Now the mother dreams of mornings not to be: eating palmed orange raspberries with her dead daughter still warm from Adam and Eve's *snake-and-apple days,* papyrus singed.

Border Lost & Found

I. Litho Wind-Up Rabbit: Tin, 1970s Vintage (Japan)
(see catalogue of unaccompanied personal effects, Item 105f)

Recall Grandmother's Flemish Rabbit Stew
(in cadence beat) with dark beer and prunes:

Item 105f

to succulent pieces of organic rabbit, she adds
vinegar, sugar, nutmeg, bay leaves and beer.

No army marches on an empty stomach!
C'est la soupe qui fait le soldat—it's soup,

or rabbit stew, that feeds the soldier,
Napoleon barks on maneuvers, gulping a gill

of diluted wine and a baguette for border-hopping,
the long loaf baked to fit into the trousers

of those famished on-the-go; no soldier escapes
the mode of self-transport (hat up!): let's move

in sync with pedetic force—the foot bounds
across the corn-shorn field; stepping in time,

the cadet's a vagabond conjuring supper:
a rabbit who becomes stew for the common good.

Both know perpetual motion best; hop-hop
goes the tin toy! This palmed wind-up rabbit

lacks the silver optimism of a wide-horizon,
a destination. It's all earnest pose and posture:

charging the line (up, up!), never crossing
a territorial border on an empty stomach.

II. Duncan Whistler Butterly Yo-Yo: Red, 1970s Vintage (USA)
(see catalogue of unaccompanied personal effects, Item 10a)

Recall Grandmother's Travel Toy for Fleeing
Noblemen of the Revolution: *émigrette*.

Item 10a

Is a wood-spinning top from 1789
too slack to mimic an émigré border jig?

Napoleon's men each pocket one
as a second heart for one splintered in battle.

Amid the draw of slip knot and spin, they wait—
and their border-hopping sovereign sobs

for troops (later) on midday patrol at Waterloo,
his cupped *bandalore* palm-side down:

it dispels the fatigue of thinking,
alleges a nervous Figaro.

Now this (re)claimed Duncan Whistler
heaves forth, like an orbiting lung,

falling and rising of its own momentum:
(up, up!) my palm's a neutral checkpoint,

a gatekeeper for a twitching Butterfly;
jou-jou doglegs past another outpost gate,

this hopping heart with string ligaments,
(relief!) red chipped and axis-spooled.

III. Babushka Chess Set: Wood, 1970s Vintage (USSR)
(see catalogue of unaccompanied personal effects, Item 53g)

Recall Grandmother's Borderless Chess Board
where inlaid mahogany squares slip

Item 53g

into infinity: no border to interrupt play;
such is the ambition of a once-sovereign, now

in exile: Napoleon's border-hopping habit
refunnels into hunting that knacky rabbit

dashing across the garden green; his pistol nudges
a clipped box hedge (aha!): a palace intruder!

Space we can recover, time never is a maxim
that drives the nighttime ritual with his aide-de-camp:

tacticians fixate on borders, since geometry cures
wanderlust and a chess board's all line and angle,

all junction and plenitude, a brute kinopolitics
of marching out the humble pawns first!

Would Napoleon—rehashing his invasion of Russia—
play on this Babushka Set? The Matryoshka's

a strategist, too, burying illicit goods in her belly:
female figurines signal an elastic equilibrium

lost at a Border Lost & Found and now
revived in a no-man's land of vintage toys

and tall tales of intersecting contractions,
then expansions—*the space we can recover.*

Tim MacGabhann

Carlos' Grandmother
From a Tape 1
Interview Location: HOLIDAY INN EL PASO
Recording Date: 30 / 12 / 12

[TV noise: audience applauds, Elvis Presley mutters his gratitude]

'Last time I saw my grandmother
she asked me
to roll her a cigarette
from the garden.
She held up her kinked fingers.
"I can't anymore."

And like, this was a whole thing.
She'd say she saw light
criss-crossing on the floor
as though thrown off lake water
coming through leaves
of the tobacco plants,
the beanstalks, the potatoes, the calabacitas —
and they weren't even there anymore.

Plus, you know, she was still funny.
When I brought her a cheese this one time,
she just moved her eyes
over its big moon-crater pores, said,
"Everybody is being so kind. I'm worried."

So I figured she was laying a prank on me
with this whole cigarette thing.
And so I slipped out,
meaning to slit open a Lucky Strike

and spill the brown shreds into one of my skins for her.
Subterfuge can be kind sometimes.
Plus, you know, I might top her joke.

But there it stood, a swaying green miracle:
the same stalk my grandad would fondle
and pull wet leathern braids from
to leave parching on the boards of the porch

while he filled his ears with the bright gauze of the air:
bird-chitter, cicada-shirr, dripping miles of trees,
his radio burbling out the football.

[lighter clicks, the wet sputtering of a bong]

'And I mean, you know, I shouldn't have been surprised.
All sorts went on there.
Grandma used to grew these orange chiles in a clay pot
to fatten on bad arguments caught in the air.

She chopped them into carnitas once, out of spite,
but the pot burst open to warn her husband,
spilled black dirt across his plate.'

[click of a can, Zippo scrapes then flares]

'After he went, her room became an El Greco sometimes,
hearts crowned with fires ringing his head
as he knelt to kiss her forehead, a living painting.

So the hank of tobacco draped on the porch-rail
no me sacó de onda. I just fibred a root-fine twist
of the stuff into a skin, licked shut the fold,

took the lit roll-up back in, and pressed it to her lips.'

A Man Walks into a Bar

From a Tape 2

Interview Location: POSADA LA PRESA, TEPOZTLÁN
Recording Date: 9 / 1 / 16

[thick slap of pool-water against tiles, filter-drone]

'For years I've tried to find life less dear to me:
the trails from plantation to cave to palenque so cold,
little in the libraries, less in the streets.
But now and then you can taste Africa —
salsa de cacahuete, stewed mats of acelga,
lard-fried triangular corn-cakes, just like the South.
One day at the market pictures rose from my plate:
my father over the skillet, Sunday morning,
tossing cracklings, from Queens via his tastebuds.
On my way back, my elbow bumped a goat's skull —
skin gone, eyes empty, every tooth sallowed by the fire.
Happier here? I don't know. Safer? Maybe.
Hearing *"negrito"* beats *"licence and registration"*,
although I wish I could hear nothing sometimes.'

[a strimmer whines, branches crunch]

'By day, on the balcony, above the pool
reflected light flashes in helices from water to tile
while a fire makes birds' bones of the hillside trees.
At night the fat pads of an iguana's feet
go clapping up along the brick.
He may well want nothing of me —
to slop a bowl of water, gobble some papaya,
to roll the seeds along his tongue like ants.
But I don't want to see him, not at all,
not the S-shapes that his shadow makes,
not his floppy, skull-to-tail mohawk of wrinkles,
not his eyes like lithographs of a dead man.
Scorpions sneak into my socks sometimes, die, dry,

skitter like rosary beads across the floor
next time I unroll a pair, but that's all, really.
Caught in a storm once, I ducked under a bridge
but got soaked anyway. Too wet to care
how heavy a zone this was for a man of my tone
I found a bar — mildewed brick, blue neon, banquettes.
A grin licked all around the room.'

[a long sigh sends up a burst of static]

'Barman's big Irish head called me *"sir"*, giggled.
Nobody was talking. Everyone was watching.
Cop memorabilia hung on the walls:
helmets, coshes, rust-blotched old photos.
When my old-fashioned slid across the bar, my eyes
were locked on the optics, on a glass case
behind the green gleam of Hennessy and Jameson — brown nubs in a
ring, spread out on green velvet
the way they'll sell you shark's teeth in tourist ports.
The barman leans in, his face a Hallowe'en-red glow,
says to me, thumb aimed at the ring, *"You know him?"*
A bead of wet rolled down my glass, down my back.
The giggles sizzled into chuckles, burst as laughs.
Those brown nubs, they were knucklebones.
In 1982. A Black man's knucklebones
kept as a cop's trophy in a New York bar.'

[deep clack of ice chunks in a glass]

'That left me one inch-wide remark away
from hearing *"You match a description."*
That'd be me toothbrushing noseblood from my chinos —
and that'd be if they left me with my blood moving.
I left the glass, nodded goodbye, let the gale
of their hoots and their laughs blow me from the room.'

[contemplative crunching of chewed ice]

One week later came my first visit here.
First man I see's a blind toting an accordion
and I have to blink frames of my Dad's town,
walking past watermelons in baby carriages,
mothers queueing to frame their daughters' diplomas,
clack and whoop from pool-halls late at night, tamales,
do-nothing Sundays, beer-crates, old folks' cane-chairs.
This town is Gaspar Yanga's last known whereabouts.
See him in a rust-splotched engraving
on a cantina wall, gaze blank as a rifle-muzzle.
A home feeling can creep up on you wherever,
and, whenever it does, better just obey.'

Hannah Linden

Bulb

He said one day it will be yellow like the sun
but first it must get used to the cold.
It's been a long time under the surface, hidden

in the back of a cupboard, forbidden
more light than it is ready to hold.
He said one day it will be yellow like the sun.

Blow it a kiss, for luck. It should be family, not one
on its own in a grey back yard. Like truth not told
it's been a long time under the surface, hidden

and alone. Love has to be strong to keep its song.
Be a trumpet, be a horn, a big brass band: unfold.
He said one day it will be yellow like the sun.

Not withered in the darkness passed father to son
and daughter, a canker that stops you getting old.
It's been a long time under the surface, hidden –

this family curse of pretend until broken.
Lass, you need light to loosen the mould.
He said one day we'll bloom yellow like the sun.
He's been a long time under the surface, hidden.

The Hole in the Cape

She takes her rest – embers into ashes,
this sleep, like red consumption – Grandma

all her life-blood sewn into this cape. Wait
until the end, she said, burn your last period

– here is your strength: let go. Forget
your father, the woodsman, the fight for a beast

inside. This is not your story. Naked or cloaked
we old women can only give you so much insight for free.

Fire and sleep war with each other. When the time
comes, your eyes stinging with smoke and tears

you will have to decide how to make your way
out of the forest. Invisibility may be more valuable

than you had thought. Grey hairs
and what seems like madness –

there are holes everywhere
if you learn how to find them.

Jack

i
My father doesn't own a name anymore.
He's just a rusty tool that has fallen
on the ground where a headstone
should be.

His workbench has collapsed in on itself.

He's flesh that's been eaten by maggots.

ii

The maggots turned into flies, laid their eggs
under my skin.

Sometimes I feel them wriggling.

Crazy right? I was a little girl,
they must all be dead by now?

No one grieves for this long.

iii

My dad got tired of building things.
All the jobs around my house wait for him
to jump back into his overalls.

In the meantime
he's holding up the sky.

iv

My dad has become a by-line:
something to sell a few books.

Everyone is going to nod, like
they know him.

Even I don't know
him. I'm not sure anyone did —

his so-called friends were shocked when he died
(his insect wings hidden under his work clothes).

v

Someone tells me he was a thief.
Someone tells me he was a saint.
Someone tells me he was Del Boy.

Someone tells me he taught himself philosophy.

They all say he was a jack-of-all-trades.
They all say he was led by his dick.
They all say he worked really hard.

vi
The buzzing comes from the walls, somewhere
near the skirting board. It sounds like there are
whole rooms full of bluebottles behind the wallpaper.

What could be so important that they can't stop?
There must be a heaven where flies go to die —
an endless round of shit ready for the taking.

Interring Grandma

i
After she died, the wolf could no longer get to her
so it was my turn to swallow her whole.

I was young so my teeth were not big. I had to take
tiny mouthfuls.

It took time to chew down the gristle of her last days.

ii
At first it felt like I was eating myself, as if I'd consumed
everything we'd ever been and made it bitter.

All I could taste was hospitals and bed-sores
and the nightmares that made her cry out
in pain.

iii
Her flesh, my flesh, more a mother
than her child-daughter ever had been

(who sends a child alone into a forest
full of wolves, her father gone?)

How to digest not being able to tell
what Grandma meant to her grandchildren
how much we loved her?

The RAF wouldn't let my brother
come to her funeral, he who she'd mothered
since he was a baby.

iv
At least I have the cape.

As the oldest she gave it to me so I'm the one
who gets to tell the story,

the one
who led the woodsman right to our door.

How Grandma adored him after that.

v
At least she never heard the rest
of the story.

She told him, with a chuckle,
to beat me if I got out of hand,

passed him the family Bible
told him to inscribe his name.

vi

The intestines were the least palatable part,
how Gran would eat tripe and pig's trotters
and tell me I should make use of everything.

She wouldn't have liked how I fact-checked the family
stories, broke their bones and sucked out the marrow.

Such lies she told to make the cottage in the wood
seem romantic. To make a wolf out of everything
she couldn't tame.

vii

And yet you can make something delicious
from the most unlikely ingredients. Take the parts
separately and it seems impossible. I try to describe
what she was like to my children but they can't
taste her unique flavour. Try and follow the recipe now
and it wouldn't work.

She's gone. Once you've picked over every crumb
washed the dishes, put them back in the cupboard
and changed where you dine, the wolf pack
turns to other prey. Isn't that how it's supposed to be?

Andrew Taylor

Song

As time leaves years behind
life's ever changing

space severs heart from heart
first love bids youthful memories

fresh affection deeper fountains
spring feelings

single moment pressed softly
flowers such a constant joy

impassioned tide ill designed
little cared for but the hour

was gratified summer skies &
sunny smiles shade severe

solemn sweetness deluge of
distress to join the broken chain

& wake the ancient flame
turn to that magic sound

that busy hum of social sound
mirrors mimics nature

Time's warning finger a score
of years departing starless nights

August 27–November 9, 1837. Patrick Branwell Brontë
April 5–April 8, 2022. Andrew Taylor

[Well! I will lift my eyes once more]

Western heaven closed
    sever thoughts wild world of misery
bright journeyer companion of dark
    decline behind native flee following west

Native home memory lost in unclouded blaze
    central light crowns dim hills though life
is waning low heart expanding
    lips frame farewell smile celestial glow

summer clouds sunlit trees blackbird's song
    bed of farewell pain wildered maze
dreamlike skies strange unsteady light
    know not the reality lost bird stormy sea

no hope in that dark air homeward through
    that wintry sky return lost bird return
glimpses of a spirit shore strength of eyesight
    to seize the falling rein through dreams

with feigned reality tossed & fevered bed
    mirror broken on grass wild dreams of western
skies & shattered memories glitter through
    the gloam in cold decay unclouded light

decline glistening gaze golden in the gleam
    as the wild winds sink in peace glorious
skies dreamy depths of azure blue sunset isles
    of paradise in cloud land

February 9, 1837. PBB
March 27, 2022. AT

Misery Part I

Bare & groaning boughs
    very energy of soul
mystery undefined
    soft & calm

December 18, 1835 PBB
March 20, 2022 AT

Rochelle Owens

from Patterns of Animus Part 4

Carnal/Spiritual

"But how could you live and have
no story to tell"

1.

The rhythm of spontaneous
change moving back and forth evokes
the scenic order

Earth Air Fire Water

Long ago   an hour ago
only a minute   morning to evening
evening to morning

Past Present Future

Cold at dawn warm
at midday boiling at midnight
a course of events moving

Back and forth every day

Bears the data data
of body body of data with each
breath a sucking sound

Animal soul Spiritual hole

Biomorphic geomorphic
polymorphic moisture and nutrients
flow in your mammalian brain

Slashes of solar light

Vibrating subatomic particles
split vertical/horizontal chasms
and fissures in the earth

Work is a binding obligation

Black and hot my coffee

Disease Famine Torture War   2

"Stupidity is brief and artless---
intelligence squirms and hides itself."

2.

On the monumental screen
an amalgam of letters join together
organize themselves

Vertical/horizontal

Moving back and forth
a jagged black line zigzags splits
zigzags breaks apart zigzags

A latent image appears

Disappears your eyes move
constantly while reading Body of Data
Data of Body

Digital letters spell

G E N U S evolution is smart
clear and simple   competition is intense
between species

Networks of neurons

Chemical molecular   a flow
of hormonal forces   hungry or thirsty
eat or drink

Sight   Smell   Taste

Digital letters spell
B A C T E R I A   S A L T   hungry
or thirsty eat or drink

Your mouth waters

Salt in the stew   salt
In the bread   your body sways
from side to side
Inhaling exhaling   3

The Universe contracts
                           E X P A N D S
spirals of veins pulsate

Your tongue protrudes
from your mouth   blood in
blood out

Work is a binding obligation

Black and hot my coffee

Disease Famine Torture War

"A longing for life. It's not a matter of intellect or logic
it' s loving with one's inside with one's stomach."

3.

On the monumental screen
a jagged black line zigzags   splits
breaks apart   zigzags

An outline shapes itself

The body of the tapeworm
moving back and forth moving
back and forth along

The alimentary canal

Digital letters spell
H E A D   N E C K and chain of
S E G M E N T S

The body of the tapeworm

S E G M E N T I N G
undulating   multiple suckers and
mouths blowing kisses

Amorous the greedy seed

Craving licking sucking   4
chewing gorging   anus to mouth
mouth to anus lickety-split

Take me away from this earth

Salt in the stew
salt in the bread I could have
danced all night

Work is a binding obligation

Black and hot my coffee

Disease Famine Torture War

"Can't I simply be devoured without being expected
to praise what devours me."

4.

A latent image appears
disappears   in such a way will
events unfold leaving

Empty spaces

Morning to evening
evening to morning you are
about to play

The role of your life

Through the gaps
of your fingers moving vertical/
horizontal moving front

And back   back and forth

An amalgam of letters
moving back and forth   slowly
the letters entwine

Audible inaudible
Moving your lips
as you read from A to Z
Oh wicked world!   5

Biomorphic geomorphic
polymorphic inhaling exhaling
with each breath

A sucking sound

Body of data data
of body moving your lips
as you read

From A to Z oh wicked world!

Digital letters spell
T R E A T   D E A T H   L I K E   B I R T H
 how tightly the words hold you

Work is a binding obligation

Black and hot my coffee

Disease Famine Torture War

"Nature doesn't ask your permission it doesn't care
about your wishes or whether you like its laws or not"

Notodoris Serenae

when they pulled that sea slug
grey-green from my elbow crease
I saw scattered spots
late night lucky blue

when they pulled it
(branching moist plasm
its appendages raised for
attention) I saw

what they pulled off
left globules saliva-slow
I saw naked bellows
unreadiness a soft blob

when they raised my arm at last
I saw so much of this pale
and clingfilm a way of not
being flesh unwrapped

Gone

As in what was once a rusted nail   my father pointed to high in the wall
of the shophouse he grew up in with his seven siblings.
As in it became a mamak shop and now   *we don't know
as the one-way road system makes it hard to stop and see.
As in paint peeling on shutters of coffee shops   at traffic lights
and overhead the swish of powerlines strung pole-to-pole   with
swallows roosting   fork-tailed   wing-to-wing. Along the lorong
that no longer exists   all the people who called and   continue
to call   lai lai   walk unhurried   as if once again   they live there.

Pontianak in London

she: still and beautiful in PureGym

fans streamingpreening hair
they pumpposepush weights
they've heard the stories   if they don't

she: beautiful and silent in
                         NewCoventGarden

pomelos cast up glow
they pack fruit alreadysticky
they've heard the stories   if they don't

she: still and silent in Paperchase

pitbull calendars flicktongues
they testtear masking tape
they've heard the stories   if they don't

stop staring
look behind

they've heard the stories
they've heard stories

and none are true

what is true
stillness   barbells red tips
beauty   beetroot bleeding

silence   pressured punch
truth   holeinskull ugly
baring teeth
snapping necks like celery

(hares)

hare coursing

if I had to
no

a harvest mouse

drinking milk
from a jug

front paws
on the lip

yellow
& then hares

if I had to

****

if I had to
but no

no necessity

blood
of course

& some do

over fields
out of veins

through veins
over fields

****

there was a blind cat
called Homer

& a cat whose eyes
etched the word "fish"

into the window glass

"I didn't come to this holy island
to castrate stray cats!"

seldom angry
a rare occasion

a rare person
a rare poet

as it happened

****

know or not
know

learn
to not know

wisteria
or oranges on the vine

dear (dead) friends
I address

not just one

****

& not only one

candle flame
no

not yet
while fires persist

burning
though rain falls

****

unknowing

unknowing?
yes

****

hare coursing
negated

in an afterlife

and now?

****

Jill Jones

While Out and About

I heard a storm sweep through the drowsing suburb.
Low-key danger bathed me in an unobtrusive lilt.

I was out looking for that fellowship of lifestyle and inclusion.
I was some way southward of its habitat and wingspan.

I was a soundtrack of clues, a kitbag of samples.
I was rinsed in a secret light, which seemed to be the heart of it.

Perhaps I was some kind of souvenir, the sough of a clown
a wastrel half-shadow, self-effacing but true in its fashion.

All my dollars have been synthesised into dashes and currents.
The fix is in, full of declines and disorders.

I was still looking for that femur of brightness, in the thunder
hefting over sparse timber, my grin in its shambles.

What I Didn't Know Even When I Did

I see my shadow on the wall
as if a fraction. I wonder if it's me.

I'm a topography, not a centre, my body
sand and water, blood and rust.

I peel clothes into the washing machine
my skin, a free space for thinking.

My memory is a many-sided room
of light and increments, folds and shade.

My animal gist leans into concrete, wood
and clay. I'm still disorganised.

At the window are other secrets
bent in small but vigilant ways.

Sweeping

My head should be lighter today
Deflation is a form of rest
I had my hair cut yesterday
Things always look different in a mirror

I swept the path today
Tidiness does achieve something
My clothes are cleaner, although it may rain
Cleanliness is normal, just as it's not

I'm not sure I quite get Verdi's Requiem
Taste isn't inevitable in this weather
The house has made a lot of sudden noises today
Indifference is a way to hide

Deflation is a kind of tidiness
I'm too dizzy to go out walking
Being dizzy, I think, has gone out of fashion
I'm not sure what I need to make a clean break from

Something is stirring in matter
I should put on a clean shirt and stand up
Let's see what happens
Let a little something unravel

Double Walking

I'm looking back at myself in a hair-pin bend.
I should open the other packet.
I float like a persona someone forgot to paint.
I am still that person who stayed, a pulse
in the space of doubt. I speak as I'm found, behind
doors to rooms I cannot enter.
Everyone lies about sex, even me, in my sleep.
My hands are empty and the little fingers are crooked.
Anger is something I find coursing through
my drinks, my homilies, my salads, my screens.
I can tell they're coming, the asteroids, the viruses,
the replicants, the future's humans. They are greedy. So am I.
I'm no more uncanny than a shadow.
There's too much clothing.

My selves all shimmer in the mirrors of the changing room.
I should get myself another body.
I move like someone who's waiting to be posed.
I am still that person who left, always
at the wrong time, dishonest about clocks and amends.
I will never get through the gates, the holy ones
or the unholy ones.
Everyone lies about the past even if it's the future.
My hands are empty and the little fingers are crooked.
I'm intemperate as a psychic wound over-described
in an airport novel. They say earth was once blissful,
but for whom? The boy gods? The trilobites or worms?
I'm no more uncanny than a shadow.
Too, too much surrounds me.

Denis Harnedy

Esker

In the days of dark subglacial miracles,
under pressure of ice,
water sometimes flowed uphill.

I walk round Lucan,
past the Marian grotto on Dodsborough Road
near the bus stop.

It is dusk and
listless people wait for the bus,
their facemasks already on.

An older person presses their hands and forehead
to the rock at the base of the grotto.
I am embarrassed and look ahead.
I don't know their gender.

What quickening happens now?
Do I walk the route of a subglacial tunnel?
Would a flame reveal pure fluid
rushing past walls of ice?

Anniversary

I drew close without love,
but love can come from nothing,
like flies from rotting meat,
like frogs from the mud on the banks of the Nile,
like children from the dead earth.

Formed heartless,
they know not what they lack,
but sometimes there is something missing,
something they might feel but don't,
something withdrawing when it should be coming close,

something about to collapse,
the Nile about to break its banks,
their parents' silence,
the tension of a fight cut short.
And isn't this how it worked in the past anyway?

Love had nothing to do with it.
And we are where we are
and I would tear my heart from my chest
and give it to you
and make you whole.

Skinny Villanelle

I'm glad you've put on weight;
last time I saw you
you were disgustingly skinny.

I'm not criticising;
it's just an observation.
I'm glad you've put on weight.

Don't take it personally.
You look fine now, but
you were disgustingly skinny.

Okay, we'll talk about it later.
It's a compliment.
I'm glad you've put on weight.

Stop going on about it.
You look better when you smile.
You were disgustingly skinny.

I'm just saying.
I don't know why I said it.
I'm glad you've put on weight;
you were disgustingly skinny.

Tamar Yoseloff

Les yeux sans visage

The surgeon bends over his daughter's mangled face;
the camera turns away.

He makes her a mask, eyes wide to the world.
Her window is a cinema: the lonely train,
the dog pulling its lead, the winter tree,
the concrete pavements, the crowds.

She singles out a girl giggling into dusk,
her skirt riding up, her skin—
the surgeon will lure her in,
slice off her face, offer it to his daughter
like a velvet cloak, graft it to her greedy bones

so she may know
the brush of her hair on her cheek,
a man's fingers seared with desire.

Nothing exists that is forever
i.m. Christo Vladimirov Javacheff (1935–2020)

He started small, with cases and cans
trussed like frantic bundles people make
when forced to leave in the night
with what they can carry on their backs;
then cars, buildings, bridges, islands –
stamped with foot falls and thumbprints,
hammer blows and bullet holes –
shrouded like grave goods to be shipped
to the next world, no fixed address.
But he believed in this world,

what we choose to protect. To cloak
is to keep safe, as you would a swaddled child
handed to its mother like a gift. His gift
to us: our world under cover, hushed.

25th February 1970

Rothko took off his glasses
and the studio clouded over,
removed his shoes, his trousers

but kept his socks on,
the kind executives wear,
fine knit, black.

> In the street
> men hailed cabs, black
> patent shoes refracting light.

> Ice cracked as they clinked
> highballs by the pool
> at the Four Seasons.

The murals devoured him,
demons steering every stroke,
black on maroon.

> They lived for the cut and thrust.

He slit his right arm,
one razor-straight line,
maroon on white.

> Hostile takeovers, blood sports.

He was found in a pool of blood
six by eight feet wide.

Lucy Sheerman

from Pine Island

Wellington, Saturday, 30 June

Dearest

I have been chasing Charlotte Brontë's correspondent across the world. The forthright voice, the tactless comments, the speaking out of turn. Here is a street named after her brother, echoes of a Yorkshire landscape I grew up in. The lady on the bus shows me where to get off: 'There's nothing to stop you crossing the world. It doesn't mean anything, does it?'

I walk up and down Cuba Street looking for the shop Mary ran with Ellen, working through the day and forgetting about dinner, prizing open packing cases filled with the goods ladies wanted and sent to her by Charlotte. *They sat on the cases and read and read. A few minutes of Nicholas Nickleby and they were asleep.* The shop assistant wants to know if there is anything he can do to help and he is not surprised when I tell him that I simply want to be here, on the site of Mary's shop. Be able to tell you of my being here.

She seemed to find no friends; instead, when a letter arrived she would pace and read in the backyard while people came into the shop, took what they wanted, and left the money. The only written record of all that long residence an advertisement for piano lessons. Charlotte's letters long-since burned, according to instruction.

Thoughts of her were unfurling far away and when she found the notice of *Shirley* in the warehouse where she bought goods for the shop she 'blushed all over'. It wasn't a place women went to, her biographer notes. She didn't know then that she was no longer her old self, had, in fact, become Rose York. How long it took for correspondence to find you out. She sends a letter to the friend she left, so many miles, so many months away. I too, will write to you.

Yours,

Wellington, Sunday 1 July

Dearest

'I began a letter to you one bitter cold evening last week, but it turned out such a sad one that I have left it and begun again. I am sitting all alone in my own house, or rather what is to be mine when I've paid for it.'

All through the night I could hear the sound of water. I didn't know if it was rain or wind or the sea out there in the darkness. All this time I have been afloat in a desert. Landlocked and the water only an idea to walk beside; the tangibility of waves out of reach although I spent all night searching. Meanwhile on the other side of the world everything is opposite – light and heat and scorched plants.

At the Wellington Museum there is a display of polished wooden spikes, smooth as tusks. Gripped by paranoia and fear of the dark, at the turn of the nineteenth century every household here owned one. As if a ship might also dock here bearing a solitary black dog and an abandoned testimony of rising terror. This place was so isolated it's no wonder they began to turn in on themselves and live in their own superstition. At a time when nothing was accidental these gleaming stakes brought a form of comfort in the midst of panic, warding off all this darkness and distance and the fear of irrevocable mistakes.

Here in Katherine Mansfield's house where guilt and sadness flow from the walls you can witness the roots of her weird realism in the Gothic. The old world haunting the new – this strange double from the old country. All the shadows cast differently in this light laced with oppositions.

'I am writing this on just such a night as you will likely read it – rain and storm, coming winter, and a glowing fire.' Darkness always encroaching on Mary's writing here in Wellington, forcing her to stop: 'You are getting too far off and beginning to look strange to me…There! it's dark.'

Yours,

Auckland, Tuesday, 3 July

Dearest

A friendship of contradictions, these letters are where the dreamer and the realist collide. The intimate confessionals are messages of tenderness sent by friends, always too far away and aware of their contingency. 'Well, it's nearly dark and you will surely be well when you read this, so what's the use of writing? I should like well to have some details of your life, but how can I hope for it? I have often tried to give you a picture of mine, but I have not the skill.'

We walked as far as the sea – hard to avoid its edges, clasping you between the sharp limit of land and that radiant sky. It's stronger here, that sense that you are only clinging on, may soon lose the strength to persevere. But it doesn't matter to us as we walk past the swimmers, sunk into the coldness of winter water. There's a little library, just an open crate, with chairs and tables on a packing case. We look through the books, searching for romance.

Last time I went to London, my companion tells me, as we arrange the books into a display, coquettish in its invitation to plummet into love again, I arrived there married and went back to Mexico divorced. She doesn't know why she was drawn to write about romance again but everyone has their own story about the pull. Is it towards a happy ever after or the anguished labour through which you earn it?

Mary only half regrets her own solitude and isolation but she chides Charlotte to end her lonely grieving and face the world again. Their long distance correspondence not enough to sustain her without other loves. Dearest, I have confided in you every detail of this journey, as I drift through these days in the strange quiet of just my own thoughts and company. Stay with me as I turn back to face the other side of the world.

Yours,

Auckland, Wednesday 4 July

Dearest

Mary knew how hard it was not to stop. How hard it was for Charlotte to keep going, bereft over the loss of her brother, her dear sisters. How much she needed hope, the urgency to write. Her answer was to keep returning to fiction. 'Look out then for success in writing; you ought to care as much for that as you do for going to Heaven.'

It seems there is always an instant when all of the practical, banal, elements of what you might call real life are shown to be contingent. Happiness, love, belief, cohere in a moment when these peripheral details, like wrapping paper, are cast aside. That's exactly when you realise the world depends on something like enchantment.

All this time you thought you were drawn to romance because of an urge to be beloved but it's only part of the answer. You should ask yourself, if desire isn't, in fact, at the heart of all these readings. The loving gaze which some people find in the idea of perfect love, others in the idea of God. If you don't want to believe in anything, the academic says, then of course that's fine. Although religion may be better than opium. At least it doesn't literally kill you.

I hoped to find you here, dearest reader, as I followed Mary, summoning you into being where before there was absence, unanswerable blank pages. Mary kept faith with writing, every letter describes the form it takes, the magic of finding something where before there was nothing. 'As to my writings, you may as well ask the Fates about that too... I never forget or get strange to what I have written.'

Yours,

Ken Bolton

For Giorgio

from lines of Tony Towle's

Hang it all, Giorgio de Chirico,
there is only the one battered faucet –
pouring out the ongoing present, in the minutes we possess.
Unstoppable. There is *no* rest.
Whether you live in Rome or Port Elliot,

there is none. Better than living in Dorset. All three tho,
bring to mind, to *my* mind, calm. Rome's traffic,
necessarily, *compels you to seek it* – a darkened room, a quiet square. Port
      Elliot suggests a certain
melancholy – but restful. And Dorset? a boarding house, a curtain
pulled against the drear sea view, the esplanade malefic –

& *empty*: dour sea wall; where lamp posts, regularly spaced,
make their unconvincing case for the decorative;
the sea itself – & the sky, just barely differentiated
from the water beneath. Time, here, is exterminated, greyed,
denied purpose. One would turn inside to a television – if

in Dorset. Let us not—in any sense of the term –
go there (*& in fact I've never been*, nor you,
Giorgio). We confine ourselves to Rome –
& Port Elliot, with its fine beach. In its South Seas bookshop a tome
devoted to your work sits, has sat for a year or more – for you

to purchase, or to rummage thru – looking for the good ones.
Ha, ha, ha. My joke. They're *all* good
one way or another. I've been thru it many times, as must have others.

(It continues to look new. 'Ish'.) The loopy ones I sort of covet…
But I have a lot at home – many a book

with works by *you*, Giorgio. My most enduring
enthusiasm. You set me on the road to loving paintings.
You, & one or two others, whom I've forgotten. ('Relegated'.)
(Nolde, Ensor.) *Then* how did it go? Munch; the contemplative
yet intense Cézanne; Matisse & Picasso – their unremitting

& inventive purpose; the great of the past – Rembrandt, Velázquez, Piero,
Raphael & Titian. The Baroque, the Rococo. My hero
Manet, & so on… Pollock. And
– who have I left out? – Kirchner, Beckmann,
… (Rauschenberg). The *minor* greats – Marquet, Filippo

de Pisis. And 'Now', … Oehlen, Christopher Wool. Time
never stands still. The faucet again. Where the element plunges out
in terrifying chunks, heavy with implication – *of your making*.
Timeless & urgent. I could *stand* beside that faucet –
lounge – metaphysical, yes – like the guy in the drawing, *The Mysterious
        Baths*.

Don't make me revisit Dorset – Bournemouth, Weymouth – I couldn't.

Dorien de Wit

translated by Judith Wilkinson

crossing

you're standing on the edge of the pavement
as if it's a cliff edge

you don't know if surrender
is a movement forward or backward

you're carrying a suitcase in your hand
but really you're clinging to it
while you're rocking on your feet

not in doubt but as a sign
of the other person inside you

someone who moves about in your body
someone who's creating a backup life
in case the first one fails

making plans
(while waiting for an overhead wire to be repaired)

building a boat that's so big
that the sea level rises
when it's launched

all the inhabitants of a continent
lift their hands up in the air at the same time
which changes the direction of the wind

making an encyclopaedia of things that don't exist

changing history
by excavating an area layer by layer
then dumping the soil back in reverse order
so that archaeologists will have to reread the past

drawing a map of disorientation

making the universe smaller
by raising as many roofs as possible
just an inch will make a difference

building a room so big that the horizon lies inside it

moving an entire village from east to west
at the speed of the earth's rotation
so that no time passes in the village

if this doesn't work

you can always move air around
by going for a walk for instance
air will instantly fill the spaces where you were

re: how are things

in the beginning there were days
I kept your unread emails in my junk mail folder
between *Mr Bill Gates says Hello,*
Michael Kors Handbags,
Hot Girls, Hello

via Google Maps I discovered the secret
an island called Mainland

for weeks I've been carrying a book in my bag
about the man who invented cloud classifications
I was so glad to discover clouds fit into a system

what do I say when I see you?
the main thing is
jumping in at the right moment
like when we skipped rope at school
and I still collected pencil shavings and found out that
popcorn is kernels of corn turned inside out

explosions are beautiful but their nature unpredictable

this country has a fault line that is growing
you said as you stared into the distance
in your eyes I saw myself and the landscape reflected
tried to figure out where the fault line started

Tom Cruise has laid down in a contract
that you're not allowed to look him in the eye
there's something in his eyes

or is it because looking
is a form of touching

Ulrike Almut Sandig

translated by Karen Leeder

Fire Earth Water Leap

Four Variations for Wilhelm Lehmann, the automatic
speech software Bruce and one's own voice

I

Fire *You*

Wilhelm
But so broken that what he wants to say is not comprehensible
Where do poems come from? Often from the impact... and the source that
emerges from it... often quite simply from something with the physical eye...
How can one ... How can one ...

Bruce
Just imagine you have been torn apart by a grenade, one would be able tell by the
label to whom all the parts flying about belonged

just imagine it was simply a game with words *You*
in the gym class of a non-partisan God
with white football shorts and a full beard
and long, hairy toes in trainers
and we were his school class of future murderers
and traitors, saviours, heroes, mothers, whingers
with perpetrator and victim indistinguishably
folded into one another and all of us barely that
first, almost memoryless, little decade old.

the Milky Way only a pigment disorder
on His forehead, His third blind eye as
he warms us children – for the Lord is
within and without, is cause, effect
blessing and curse – when he warms
the stiff little limbs of us children. FIRE!
EARTH! WATER! STORM!, He bellows and
blows his black whistle so that the little
white ball leaps up into the invisible.

at FIRE! you must fling yourself flat on the
floor, wherever you are. just imagine you will
be torn apart by a grenade if you lift your head
too high. we throw ourselves flat on our stomachs
and close our eyes to know our enemy.
he lives in our own heads and looks just like
– everything you'd expect of – us. today
our enemy has left behind his sports kit with its   *Wilhelm*
sewn-in name tags, it wasn't you. just imagine   How can one...
the whistle blows from above and you are torn apart   How can one...
by a grenade. how should i know to whom the tattered
body parts belong, without sewn-in name tags.

Wilhelm
How can one reach the depths?

II
Earth

You

Bruce
The company swarmed onto the newly ploughed field.
Bright green stems of garlic plants still standing fresh in the meagre soil. Dig in!

eingraben. digging in.
night. then rain came
in sheeves, bright ring
bleeds. benign being
goes running ragged
into rocks again. so m-
uch anger here in being
near. itch back of fear.
B calls her N. black bitch.

beginning to get in g-
ear: be gone desire. this
garbage her inner rage?
her so engaged, bare,
in range. this here is
her grave. her left afr-
aid, the rage-binge near-
ing. gave all to save. B:
'nein?' this is all staged!

eingraben? ire began
in her, growing big:
not digging in fear, not
digging a grave. light-
child she heaves, sheer
she-bear, not birthing
a slave. she bore an N.
but N's dug in deep,
no guile, lost in sleep.

whether to weep? no!
she will begin again, grin,
grab Baeren-Gin, bear it
bear again, wear her scars
inside, stars by her side,
her heart on her sleeve.
was greed, and disdain,
inner pain: face forwards
now whatever remains. B:–

III
Water

You

Bruce
Nuch fanned out with his group, threw himself down behind a thistle;
the purple head was dusted with rain.

just imagine, He does it again, although
He promised He never would, and even
pinned a rainbow under the blue ceiling

of his gym so that you would believe
him. WATER, He calls and the little white
ball of the third eye on His forehead

starts moving, and you charge off toward
the wooden benches, standing in rows
in front of the wall-bars. anyone not at the top

on count of three, He yells, in his snow-white
gym teacher's kit, has lost! just imagine how
the rain is dripping completely and without

comprehension from the ceiling and – as time
stands still and you watch the rain crashing
watch the crashing itself – it runs down your cheeks

IV
Leap   *You*

Wilhelm
How can one reach the depths, before the surface is spread out
before our eyes? There is no last without the last but one.

Bruce
And everything depended on this leap: the earth, the heavens, the people.

there is no 'just imagine' without the 'just'.

there is no first without the second.

and everything depended on these people: the leap, the earth, the heavens.

there is no gym-teacher without the class.

there is no first without the last.

and everything depended on these heavens: the people, the leap, the earth.

there are no perpetrators without the 'them'

there are no sacrifices without the 'i'.

and everything depended on this earth: the heavens, the people, the leap.

there is no last without the last but one.

there is no 'there is no' without the 'there is'.

Wilhelm
So where do poems come from?

Fire   *You*

Chen Xianfa

translated by Martyn Crucefix & Nancy Feng Liang

Graveyard Bearing No Flowers or Fruit

Halfway up the mountain there is a large graveyard,
all the turf and trees that used to cover it
uprooted, so now
nothing but the rough, brown earth is left exposed.
It's clear, even in a flourishing Spring,
this whole place will remain
without fruit or flowers.

For my old father, death is something
to be found on our side.
Some of his old clothes in the old family closet
still strive to retain his human form –
on some occasions,
they still feel warm.

As to the flowers and fruit of the world beyond this,
we have no more than endless speculation.
How many greetings from the world of extinction
ought to be remembered?
In every speck of earth that I take up in my hands,
my old father answers me,
as my old, half-deaf mother,
just now burning the rice to a cinder on the stove, also
answers me.

'As aubergines ripen'

As aubergines ripen, they grow purple-black.
The weeds on all sides
grow even more vigorously.

After being away, after travelling for two months,
I'm shocked at the sight of the garden.
Our beloved aubergines
have been completely swamped.
It turns out a world let go to be governed by no more
than simple nature is hard to take.

And yet, this frenzied blanketing never stopped the ripening.

I wonder if writing ought to lie there too,
in the now shrivelling grass, in a temperate breeze,
beside the aubergines, contemplating its own frailty,
doing away with self-pity…

'Jogging at night'

Jogging at night. I've heard it said, every year someone leaps
to their death from this apartment block.
I stop to take a closer look at the dark building.

A few lights show up above
like a lingering heartbeat.

I have felt something of the sort, jumping down
from a tall dyke. Readying to leap,
there is always a mysterious force shoving you from behind.

Then, flying through thin air. Death
achieved with no effort –

pupils rapidly dilating, in turn being pierced by flowers,
by pollen, the grains of pollen.

Good Intentions

Good intentions that do not reveal themselves are as dust.
Lakes in the evening take on an indigo hue.

Birds low down in the sky, not changing direction.
Withered grass along the shoreline, without suspicion.
After a while, elm trees become so dense only their outlines remain.

The old man who approaches me –
there is a stony coldness in his face.

And all this is hardly worth my writing it down.
The silt is dark and soft
and puts me in mind of a placenta.

I was brought up on the taste of nature's desolation,
one chewed mouthful
after another. Only intensified
by hyperbolic tower blocks in the distance, their neon lighting.

As flawless as a light frost
and like a light frost, unsustainable.

Notes on Contributors

GORDON ALEXANDER's work in this issue is his first publication.

LISA BLACKWELL is a writer of poetry, fiction and plays, and is currently in the final year of an MSt in Creative Writing at University of Oxford. Her poetry has been published by *The Rialto*, *3AM Magazine* and in the anthology, *Footprints: an anthology of new ecopoetry* (Broken Sleep Books, 2022). She also writes short fiction, and her short plays have been produced at Rich Mix, and the Chiswick Playhouse in London.

CECILE BOL is a Dutch writer with a small family and a big edible garden in the north of the Netherlands. Her debut chapbook *Fold me a Fishtail* was published by Selcouth Station Press in March 2022. Her work has also appeared in several online journals, magazines and anthologies. Cecile leads a local English poetry stanza. She owns 57 different kinds of herbs and spices of which cumin and dill are her favourites.

KEN BOLTON is an Australian poet, whose *Selected Poems 1975–2010* (2012) and *Species of Spaces* (2018) were published by Shearsman Books. His most recent collection is *Fantastic Day* (Puncher & Wattman, Sydney, 2021). He is based in Adelaide.

JESSICA BUNDSCHUH is a lecturer at the University of Stuttgart in English Literatures and Cultures and holds a Ph.D. in Creative Writing and English Literature. Her poems have appeared in *The Paris Review* and *The Los Angeles Review*. Current work appears *The Moth Magazine*, *Long Poem Magazine*, and *The Honest Ulsterman*.

CHEN XIANFA [陈先发] is a prize-winning poet and journalist, born in Anhui Province, China. He has published five books of poems, including *Poems in Nines* (2018; bilingual Chinese/English, tr. Nancy Feng Liang) which was awarded the Lu Xun Prize. A *Selected Poems* appeared in 2019. He has also published two collections of essays, *Heichiba Notes* (2014 and 2021).

GERALDINE CLARKSON has two chapbooks from Shearsman, one of them (*Declare*) a Poetry Book Society choice, and a first collection, *Monica's Overcoat of Flesh* from Nine Arches Press (2020). Verve published her most recent chapbook, *Crucifox*, in 2021, and a further full collection, *Medlars*, is forthcoming from Shearsman.

MARTYN CRUCEFIX's recent publications are *Cargo of Limbs* (Hercules Editions, 2019) and *The Lovely Disciplines* (Seren, 2017). *These Numbered Days*, translations of Peter Huchel (Shearsman Books, 2019) won the Schlegel-Tieck Translation Prize, 2020. He has also translated for Enitharmon, and has published *Daodejing* – a new version in English (Enitharmon, 2016). A Rilke *Selected* will be published by Pushkin Press in 2023. His translation of essays by Lutz Seiler, *Sundays I Thought of God*, is due from And Other Stories in 2023. He is currently a Royal Literary Fund Fellow at The British Library and blogs on poetry, translation and teaching at www.martyncrucefix.com

ANGELINA D'ROZA has had poems in various journals, including *Poetry Review*, *The Honest Ulsterman*, and *Blackbox Manifold*. Work has also been included in anthologies from publishers such as Smith/Doorstop, Boiler House Press and in the Sheffield edition of Dostoyevsky Wannabe's Cities series. Her first collection was released by Longbarrow Press in 2016, and a pamphlet, *Correspondences*, was published by Longbarrow in 2019.

NANCY FENG LIANG is a bilingual poet and translator living in Massachusetts and North Carolina. She has translated Henry David Thoreau's *Wild Fruits* into Chinese (Culture and Development Press, 2018) and Chen Xianfa's *Poems in Nines* (Anhui Education Press, 2018). Her most recent poetry collection, *Qi Cun Tie*, was published by Taiwan Showwe Press, 2020. She graduated with a Master's from Harvard in 2004.

LUCY HAMILTON works freelance for Cam Rivers Publishing. She has two books with Shearsman, and is currently working on a collection which draws upon her experiences in China, and on the *I Ching*. Poems from this project have appeared in *Tears in the Fence, Shearsman, Artemis, The Fortnightly Review*, and *Stand*. She is also working on a third collection of prose poems.

DENIS HARNEDY is a barrister living and working in Dublin. He has recently begun writing poetry, inspired by his year of living in a suburb of Dublin, and the experiences he had there. Before training in law, he worked as an English-language teacher in China where he developed a love of Chinese, and especially Tang-dynasty, poetry.

FINN HAUNCH is a poet based in Newcastle-upon-Tyne. His writing has been published in *Ink, Sweat & Tears* and *Dark Mountain*. He is interested in the connections between psychology and theology, as well as the culture and history of Northern England.

JILL JONES is an Australian poet, with thirteen full-length books of poetry, including *Wild Curious Air*, winner of the 2021 Wesley Michel Wright Prize, and *A History Of What I'll Become*, shortlisted for the 2021 Kenneth Slessor Award. Her work has been translated into many languages, including Chinese, French, Italian, Czech, Macedonian and Spanish.

L. KIEW is a London-based poet of Chinese-Malaysian heritage. She works as a charity-sector leader and accountant. She holds an MSc in Creative Writing and Literary Studies from Edinburgh University. Her debut pamphlet was *The Unquiet* (Offord Road Books, 2019). She was a 2019/2020 London Library Emerging Writer and is currently working on her first collection.

EDWARD LEE's poetry, short stories, non-fiction and photography have been published in magazines in Ireland, England and America, including *The Stinging Fly, Skylight 47, Acumen* and *Smiths Knoll*. His play *Wall* was part of Druid Theatre's Druid Debuts 2020. His debut poetry collection *Playing Poohsticks On Ha'Penny Bridge* was published in 2010. He also makes musical noise under the names Ayahuasca Collective, Lewis Milne, Orson Carroll, Blinded Architect, Lego Figures Fighting, and Pale Blond Boy.

KAREN LEEDER is a writer, critic and translator of German literature who teaches German at the University of Oxford. Her translation of Ulrike Almut Sandig's *Thick of it* (Seagull Books, 2018) won an English PEN award and an American PEN/Heim award. Her translation of Sandig's *I am a field of rapeseed, give cover to deer and shine like thirteen oil paintings laid one on top of the other* (Seagull Books, 2020), was shortlisted for the Oxford Weidenfeld Prize, 2021 and longlisted for the ALTA Translation Prize, 2021.

HANNAH LINDEN is widely published and recently won the Cafe Writers Open Poetry Competition 2021. She is working on a first collection, *Wolf Daughter*, about the impact on children of parental suicide; the poems here are all drawn from this manuscript. Her pamphlet *The Beautiful Open Sky* is due shortly from V. Press. Twitter: @hannahlin

TIM MACGABHANN was born in Kilkenny, Ireland, and began his writing career as a music journalist while studying English Literature and French at Trinity. Since 2013, he has reported from all over Latin America. His critically-acclaimed debut novel *Call Him Mine* was a *Daily Telegraph* 'Thriller of the Year' in 2019. His fiction, non-fiction, and poetry has appeared in *Gorse*, *The Stinging Fly*, and *Washington Square*, and he holds an M.A. in Creative Writing from the University of East Anglia. He lives in Mexico City.

AONGHAS MACNEACAIL is a leading voice in Gaelic poetry: in the Highlands, he is still widely known as 'Aonghas Dubh' ('Black Angus'). In Glasgow, he became part of Philip Hobsbaum's writing group which included Alasdair Gray, James Kelman, Liz Lochhead and Tom Leonard. His work has been described as a bridge in Gaelic poetry 'between the old and the new, the literary and the vernacular, Scotland and the world.' His last English-language collections, *Rock & Water* (1990) and *laughing at the clock : new and selected poems* (2012) were both published by Polygon, Edinburgh.

DAVID MILLER's Collected Poems, *Reassembling Still* was published by Shearsman Books in 2014, and his *Afterword* was also published here this year.

ELIZA O'TOOLE has a PhD from the University of Essex where she walked among experimental poets of note. She has an abiding anxiety about the perception of the nature of land, led by language. Her second collection of poetry, *The Formation of Abscission Layers*, will be published in 2023 by Muscaliet Press, and includes the poems printed here.

A central figure in the international avant-garde for fifty years, **ROCHELLE OWENS** is a poet, playwright, translator, and video artist. She has published 17 books of poetry including *Hermaphropoetics, Drifting Geometries* (Singing Horse Press, 2017), *Out of Ur: New & Selected Poems 1961–2012* (Shearsman Books, 2013), *Solitary Workwoman* (Junction Press, 2011), and *Luca: Discourse On Life And Death* (Junction Press, 2001).

PETER RILEY's *Collected Poems* is available from Shearsman Books, in two volumes.

ULRIKE ALMUT SANDIG has written five volumes of poetry and two volumes of short stories. Her new novel *Monsters like us* appeared in English this year. She is a notable performer and has won many prizes, including most recently the Erich Loest Prize and the Roswitha prize (both 2021). She lives with her family in Berlin.

These four poetic variations are based on extracts and ideas from the autobiographical novel *Der Überläufer* (The Deserter) by Wilhelm Lehmann (1882–1968) best known as a nature poet. Written in 1927 and published only in extract in the early 1960s, it is now considered one of the most radical anti-war novels in the German language. This wide-ranging text explores the war that marks the end of German colonial history. Hanswilli Nuch, a sensitive middle-aged academic, is called up in the closing year of the war and encounters the brutality of the military. Trying to escape its bogus solidarity and toxic hierarchies, Nuch risks his life by deserting; his 'leap' out of the trench finally allowing him to cross over to the British army. Extracts from the novel are spoken by Bruce, named after an automated speech computer program. The piece also includes quotations from Lehmann's 1957 radio essay *Gespräch über Bäume* [A Conversation about Trees]. Sandig produced *Fire Earth Water Leap* in 2018 together with her sound-cosmonaut Sebastian Reuter as a short radio play.

LUCY MAXWELL SCOTT is working on a collection of poems about the life of Rosa Luxemburg. She has previously had poetry published in *Frosted Fires First* (Cheltenham Festival) *Ink Sweat and Tears, Interpreters House, Tears in the Fence,* and the *Morning Star* newspaper. She has been long- and short-listed for various poetry competitions, including the National Poetry Prize 2020.

LUCY SHEERMAN runs the Creative Writing Centre at the Institute of Continuing Education, University of Cambridge where she also teaches. Previously she worked as literature officer at Arts Council England, helping to establish the National Centre for Writing.

PENELOPE SHUTTLE has lived in Cornwall since 1970. Her first collection of poems, appeared from Oxford University Press in 1981, and was followed by six other Oxford books, and then four individual collections and a retrospective volume from Bloodaxe. *Redgrove's Wife* (2006) was short-listed for both the Forward Prize and the T.S. Eliot Prize in 2006. Recent collections include *Lyonesse* (Bloodaxe Books, 2021), and *Heath,* a collaboration with John Greening, (Nine Arches, 2016).

SOPHIE (JIANGHONG) SONG was born and grew up in China. She worked as public relations coordinator in Xiamen University and had a part time job as radio presenter in Xiamen Economic and Transportation Station. She now works for Cam Rivers Publishing, and lives in Cambridge with her husband and two children.

ANDREW TAYLOR has published three collections with Shearsman Books, the latest being *Not There—Here* in 2021. He recently edited Peter Finch's *Collected Poems* for Seren Books. He lives and works in Nottingham. www.andrewtaylorpoetry.com

JUDITH WILKINSON is a British poet and translator. She grew up in the Netherlands and is fully bilingual, but she translates exclusively into English. She now lives in Groningen, the Netherlands. In addition to writing her own poetry, she translates contemporary Dutch and Flemish poetry. Among the poets whose work she has translated into English are Toon Tellegen, Miriam Van hee, Menno Wigman and Hagar Peeters. Shearsman Books published her edition of Menno Wigman's *The World by Evening* in 2020.

DORIEN DE WIT is a Dutch poet and visual artist. Her first collection, *eindig de dag nooit met een vraag* (never end the day with a question), from which these translations were taken, gained her immediate recognition as an original new voice on the Dutch poetry scene. The book was nominated for the prestigious C. Buddingh prijs. In this collection she explores what 'place' means, and where the 'I' is in relation to the other, in situations that seem in every way uncertain.

TAMAR YOSELOFF's poems in this issue will all appear in her next collection, *Belief Systems,* due from Seren in 2023.